Flowers in the Sunshine

Flowers in the Sunshine

Sarbajit Roy

ZB

ZORBA BOOKS

ZORBA BOOKS

Published by Zorba Books, May 2021
Website: www.zorbabooks.com
Email: info@zorbabooks.com

Cover design© Sithesh
Copyright © Sarbajit Roy

ISBN Print Book - 978-93-90640-57-7
ISBN eBook – 978-93-90640-58-4

Zorba Books Pvt. Ltd. (opc)
Sushant Arcade,
Next to Courtyard Marriot,
Sushant Lok 1, Gurgaon – 122009, India

B-315, Okhla Industrial Area, Phase 1, New Delhi- 110020

Dedicated to
My Father Mother and Brother
and to those who always remain in my mind as dreams of the past

Acknowledgements

Poetry is drawn from the fonts of inspiration and there are many of my personal friends and near ones who have provided much encouragement and constant words of inspiration .My sincere gratitude to all who have provided constant support to my writing.

My sister, Saswati Jana, who writes poems regularly and has published with the West Bengal Sahitya Academy has constantly inspired me to continue writing .I am also grateful to my sister's family, and maternal brother-in-law Prosanto Roy Chowdury and other relatives for their constant support.

One of my WhatsApp groups, who consist of my ex colleagues from Ghatsila , each of them distinguished in their respective fields, have been a fantastic source of support .I have posted poems frequently in the group and have been fortunate to receive accolades from every one of them.Supriyo Roy , Abhijit Chakravarty, ,Dipankar Chakravarty, Arun Roy, Kushal Ghosh, Shubhendu Bhattacharya, Amal Ghosh, Bhaskar Bhattacharya Anup Roy Chowdhury, Anupam Dutta and Arup Dutta have delightedly given me very encouraging reviews.

I am also indebted to Mrs. Iris Kemier Burnham , my ex employer for many years in El Paso, Texas, USA.Mrs. Burnham has repeatedly given me excellent reviews and unabated words of encouragement for many years. She is a well known Academic entrepreneur in El Paso, has taught English and literature for more than forty years, and also a senior member of the Democratic Party in the city of El Paso and the State of Texas.

My acknowledgments to faculty and students of my present Institution , who have also urged me to write further. Among the faculty , I would like to express heartfelt thankfulness to Sailesh Pandey , Purushottam Kumar, Consultant Vishal Kumar and Abhay Singh for their constant motivation .

My sincere gratitude to the Management a d owners of the Institution Chairman Ravindra Kumar and Treasurer Romus A. for constantly inspiring me and providing g ambient and wonderfully verdant natural surroundings that have ushered the finest feelings for composition .

My sincere gratitude to many others who have send their likes towards my poetry in Facebook. The list is long and exhaustive,.A special .mention must be made of my childhood and schoolfriend Subhashish Purakayastha, who lives in Boston , USA who has constantly supported me in many areas.My school friends, Monotosh Bakshi, Verghese Kunjachan, Pradeep Prasad, Dev Mukherjee ,Tirtha Mukherjee, have assisted and sent me tokens of inspiration.Parveen Chatbar and Juzar Sitabkhan have motivated through facebook.My close friends in El Paso, Mansoor Ahmed and Vishnu Shankar have been a constant support during my entire stay for more than 25 years in El Paso Texas.

I would lgratefully ike to thank others who have supported me constantly .

Finally, I would like to express my gratitude to Zorba Books for their untiring efforts to produce a quality product. My special thanks Zorba Books team who gave me much encouragement and who have strived to make this publication a success.

Preface

This book is a collection of poems I have written over a long period of time. One of my early inspirations has been drawn from my father's writings, who never published any of his poems, but was a class writer. Themes of nature and surroundings have remained an integral part of the content. Many poems in this collection have been written with flashes of insight and revealing visions of Nature.

Every poem is an expression in words of a picture, framed in its entirety. A person or character such as "The old barber", "An elderly lady ", or "The maidservant " brings forth vivid details through poetic lines. The themes chosen are varied and always colorful. Abstract topics such as "The mind" and "Flow of time " have been given creative details that were embedded in the poet's mind. Visual depictions of "A stream in the woods" and "The path to the woods" evolves into picturesque motion, with detailed surroundings.

Poetry remains in the mind as lucid as dreams, and every description in this collection hopefully creates a clear picture.

I express my sincere gratitude to all readers for their interest.

Contents

Flowers in the Sunshine

As sunshine streams into the garden of delight,
The birds sing with incessant song,
Bees murmur, to butterflies in flight,
The balmy breeze blows the flowers along;

Every flower smiles a unique smile,
Rays of the sunshine in unabated thrill,
Leaves rustle in the soft wind every while,
Glorious happiness on the flowers does nature instill;

Life pulsates through the garden beds in glee,
Streams of music spring from the soil towards the sky,
An incoming joy spreads through every flower laden plant and tree
And floats with the birds as higher they fly .

The Lonely Tree

One beautiful morning, as I walked solitary and free,
Along rambling roads and detours dark,
I came across a lonely tree
On grassy landscape endless and stark;

Clouds descended on the horizon of gold,
And gathered around the far hilly slopes,
Wrapping them in their subtle fold,
The mist and breeze obscured sunshine's hopes;

A pond on the edge of the dusty roads,
Where lotuses floated in sparkling blaze,
Shelter for birds, who flew in hordes,
Watched by the tree's unearthly gaze;

Women carrying lumber on their sturdy heads,
Swayed with balance, along the path with spree,
A stray dog slumbered on its dusty bed,
Under the shade of the lonely tree;

Six little puppies nestled, their mother near
Each rolling and playing with its little sibling friend,
Born in the wild, with little fear,
Such joy and vigor did they to the tree lend;

Lonely tree, for eons have you stood,
And watched the world and time fly pass,
Your roots have rested in the soil so good,
And nourished the dew in the growing grass .

The village road

As I walked along the village road,
Past ploughed fields and shady green,
My hopes and heart above soared
When I saw the smile of a child so lean;

In her hands was a little branch of a tree
To guide the goats to their shelter and home,
From the fields where the buffaloes graze free,
And the little goats with their mothers roam;

Barefoot she ran with her little brother beside,
As gossiping women on the roadside sat,
The little boy with his eyes so wide,
Saw the world in a haze somewhat;

Children joined and ran along,
She smiled her carefree, shining smile,
The goats pranced, as if dancing to a song,
The village elders gazed all the while;

Far from the mansioned rich she lives and plays,
In rustic lands where sunshine is free,
Her shabby dress is rich in life always,
Her village the abode of freedom be;

O village road, lead me there
Where humans share with creatures all,
Poverty melts in the heart so fair;
And blessings of nature arrive at every call.

Discovery

Brave were the hearts that sailed
Over forbidden depths, waters
Dark and foreboding. turbulent seas
In search of novel lands ;
Into the cold extremities of the earth
Where kingdoms of ice held sway:
Into tropical forests, where
Monuments of lost civilizations
Lay hidden, under dense undergrowth,
Standing as mute testimonies
Of forgotten glories ;
Into windswept desert sands
Where mummified humans
Attempt to defy death;
Into the top of the world
Surveying the hazy landscape below
Through porous clouds;
Into the abysmal waters of oceans,
Peering into strange creatures
Through glass windows;
Seeing with the eyes of Columbus
Vistas of new worlds,
The modern-day explorers
Venture into space,
A limitless frontier -
The first faltering steps
Like a toddlers,
Leads to the moon,
And thence to Mars ;
The Solar system and beyond
Lie in wait, the galaxy

With its hundred billion stars
Among hundred billion galaxies
Await the footsteps of mankind;
The universe amidst other universes,
Worlds within worlds
Wait for eternity ;
The dreams of discovery
Travel their reveried paths.

Silence

Beauty shines outside my window,
The soft breeze past the swaying leaves
Leaves but a note of transient pleasance
Till the dying wind heaves a final gust -
Then silence engulfs all sounds except its own,
Tender murmurs of rosebuds disappear into the stillness,
Golden silence, pervading the unfathomable depths of the ocean
Strikes eloquence into its teeming tenants;
The evening rays of the declining sun
Imbues the tranquil air with words,
These are the words we spoke
When the world was fragile and young,
These are the words we will speak
When the world is no more.

Twilight

Twilight, as the golden orb does descend
Towards the distant horizon and below,
Shadows of darkness shall transcend
The stars, and set silver moonlight aglow;

As the tree-lined landscape fades from sight
And majestic silence reigns supreme,
Fireflies appear, clad in garments bright,
Shadowy boats sail the river to the land of dream;

Incessant chirps of crickets, the lonely bark of a dog,
A baby's distant cry, in its mother's arms,
Cattle returning home, through the evening fog,
The cool breeze flowing through the quiet farms;

In reverence to the conflux of night and day,
When life and time stand solemnly still,
The earth and sky whisper away,
And twilight gleams on the distant hill.

My window

From my window I can splendidly see
The first rays of the sun so soft,
Striking the leaves of the stately tree
And the feathers of the bird that sails aloft;

I see cows grazing on the grassy green,
Flowers smiling with radiance in the lustrous light,
Clouds sailing to kingdoms before unseen,
The hills beyond a shining sight;

With faltering steps, the little child walks
Towards the gates of her house to see
The world beyond, the panorama of life talks
In garbled language and actions so free;

The twilight I watch from my window clear
As golden hues of the setting sun
The sky and clouds with paint endear,
Nature›s elegance is never undone;

At night when through my window beams
The moon and stars› soothing light,
Dream and vision in silence streams
Into the mind, lucid and bright;

Window of my mind, window of my heart,
Through your hallowed portals, this Self sets sail
To worlds of bliss does it blessedly depart,
My window does the Immortal Spirit hail.

Egypt forever

Across the banks of the Nile,
Voices from the centuries speak,
Echoing over the towering pyramids
And the intriguing sphinx ;
As the primordial rays of dawn
Strike the obelisks at Karnak,
Amun appears from his sanctuary
Garbed in golden robes ;
Whispers reverberate between the pylons
And disappear far away
Inside the Valley of Kings ;
The spirits of Pharaohs rise
To mingle with eternity ;
The eyes of Horus guard the tombs
Etched with images of forever ;
Anubis gazes on, with jackal eyes
Gleaming in the darkness
Of the chamber;
The search for eternal life
Goes on in the listless desert.
The lotus blooms over the primeval waters
In a cycle of renewal;
Tutankhamen, Hatsepshut, Thutmosis, Ramses
Parade with their shaven-headed priests
Across the bridges of time;
Old, Middle and New Kingdoms
Merge in space;
Cleopatra, in her palace below the sea
Welcomes the chariots of Ra
Which race across the dusty roads
Of Alexandria, Cairo, Giza and Thebes.

A better world

Let us build a better world
A world where all can share,
Where the flag of humanity is unfurled,
And there is love everywhere ;
O, a world where no child
Goes hungry on any day,
Rain or storm, harsh or mild,
A shelter stands, come what may ;

Let us build a kinder place
Where education is always free,
For every child, of every race
Who shall receive knowledge with glee;

Let us build a world in freedom's wake
Where quest for power and greed,
Shall not the leader's character make,
But respect for every caste, color or creed ;

Let us strive to build an earth
Without hate, apathy and war,
Where every person has a golden worth
And a vivid dream to live for ;

Let us build a shining land
Where future generations can say,
"We live in a world where we proudly stand,
Because our forefathers showed us the way ."

The path through the woods

A temple near the woods I have seen,
A path worn down by hundreds of years
Leading to the forest foliage, dense green,
And this I traveled allaying all my fears;

Tribals traveled the path for lumber,
Which sustains their fires at home,
Small animals awoke from their slumber
And scurried to hide as the people did roam;

The trees in mute silence did every move sense
Birds raised a low, constant voice,
A lonely fox bounded across the fence
And hid in the brushes without further choice;

Wildflowers swayed in the restless breeze,
Large leaves spread their colored show,
Butterflies settled on branches of trees,
A peacock hurried, its crest stooping low;

The path to the woods is quiet and clear
A soothing silence my mind does know,
 The road stretches far with no dwelling near,
As I walk through the woods with steps so slow.

Distant realms

I asked the traveller, "Where do you go?"
With a smile, he replied, " I do not know ;
The miles I travel to distant realms,
My heart rejoices, my mind overwhelms."

Noble Goddess

Noble goddess, symbol of virtue, wisdom emanates
From your being,
Your first war cry delivered
When you sprung from mighty Zeus›s head
In full armor, full-grown,
Was heard over every meadow and mountain of Greece,
Rejuvenating the glistening snows of Mount Parnassos,
Striking terror and awe
Into the hearts of mortals and gods alike,
Placated Zeus honors you with his indomitable aegis,
The petrifying head of Medusa in the midst
Fringed with serpents
And the mighty spear blazing thunderbolts
Overland and sea ;
Hellenes and Trojans,
Athenians and Amazons,
Centaurs and Lapiths,
Gigantes and Olympians,
You emerge the architect of victory ;
Bright-eyed Pallas Athene, Incarnate wisdom   prudence
and effulgent purity,
Creator of the bridle, flute, plow and ship,
Protectress of cities, of heroes and fragile men,
Pericles, Athens, Greece and the world pay homage
To your towering presence
At the precincts of the Parthenon
Where Phedias toiled with enraptured marble,
Gold and ivory;
Nike and sharp spear on either hand,
Sphinx and Pegasus -like horse adorning the helmet,
Coiled serpent near sandals of gold,

Shield resting beside the feet,
Tranquility residing in eyes of gemstone
And along the golden drapery -
Athena Parthenos,
You stand triumphant, ushering peace,
Dispelling the darkness of disorder.

Atlantis

Atlantis! You awaken in people's minds
A utopia! Our dreams fulfill
A part of ourselves - we yearn for the higherr,
Yet, resplendent in all our glories
We fall, from our highest pedestals -
Paragons Of civilization, yet so frail,
History replete with fallen heroes, fallen kingdoms -
Even mighty Rome - the Eternal City, burnt to embers,
Be it Poseidon's wrath, or Zeus's curse,
You remain, the ultimate myth of the world.
If Thera be your hunting grounds,
The blast of a thousand Krakatoas
Did never obliterate you from our minds -
Civilizations of the past, and of the future
Shall reminisce of you and place your achievements
Even loftier than theirs.
Your existence lost in the mists of time
Shall continue to inspire poets and
Tales of your exploits
Repeat till time immemorial.

Kolkata by night

Kolkata smiles as descends upon her the night,
On streets, lanes, boulevards and the flyovers long,
Vehicles and humans move under the glittering night,
The pensive air is filled with a perennial song ;

The Shahid Minar stands in mute splendor,
The Howrah Bridge shines over the waters still,
On lighted Park street walk sojourners in quiet grandeur,
On Esplanade, the din from crowds does the air fill;

Street dwellers make their crude beds under the stars,
Restaurants cater to their customers and their orders fill,
Malls flash neon lights and sell their quality wares,
Street hawkers shout in voices loud and shrill;

Victoria Memorial with the fairy on its crest,
Lit in splendor, watches vintage horse carriages roll,
Their hooves stirring the dust of centuries do not rest
They stir the city›s heritage and its imprisoned soul;

College Street, inundated with books of every kind,
The Coffee House with discussions on every topic sublime,
Rouse and invigorate the aspired mind
To soar into creative thoughts in every clime;

Behind a sprawling tree an old mansion looms,
Once a landlord›s abode, its heydays of glamour now faded,
Creaking windows and doors, empty and dark rooms,
Stare in eerie silence, amidst ornate pillars now jaded;

Trams travel at crawling speeds on tracks laid decades past,
Metro trains travel at fast pace with the commuters› homeward crowd,
Modernity mingles with traditions old and outcast,
Affluence and poverty in harmony meet the free and the proud;

The river flows in silent ripples, along its timeless shores,
A witness to history, which memory does never leave,
Spellbound is the traveller, as time opens its doors,
O Kolkata, what infinite magic forever do you weave!

The dew-drenched bud

A dew-drenched bud in bloom
On a sapling beside the rocky edge of a garden,
Life has sprung with the sunshine of the morning
To be nourished by the earth and
The radiant sun, as spring attired in color
Spreads over the verdant grass
And blends with the leaves which embed the bud;
The proud sapling hears the praise of the birds,
The clouds float gracefully in the clear sky,
Life blooms, to grow into an alluring flower,
Collecting joys and dispelling griefs,
With its facelifted to the skies
As the heart hopes for a future as bright.

The essence of life

Life that flows through veins of ours,
Flows too in every blade of grass,
Life blooms in all fragrant flowers,
And every creature that comes to pass;
The rhythms of life beat in every tree,
Life radiates from each ray of the sun,
Full of life every little bacteria be,
All life on earth is unified in one;
Life is a mirror, the spirit its grace,
Life is vibrant, and living is its goal,
The beauty of the mind does life embrace,
The essence of life is the eternal soul.

The elderly Lady

Chiselled as in stone, a stoic face,
Worn, wrinkled with age and time,
She squatted near the market place
In graceful splendor, past her prime ;

A smile of mystery over her profile did pass
As perhaps she recollected her bygone years,
Folds of thought on her temple did amass,
In memory of moments of joy and tears;

To a transient future her mind rested upon,
Uncertain, yet reserved in earthly space,
Her random memories flashed off and on,
She sat in silence, in benign grace;

The river of life before her quietly flows,
Hours gradually pass and days slowly stretch,
Her mind wanders the world, each eye avidly glows,
The elderly lady is a portrait time does patiently sketch.

Forgotten melody

Who could tell the flapping bird in the cage
That spring is far away? Guardians of music who
Have filled the world with song
Did not wait to hear
The doleful melody
Of the forgotten bird;
Sweet sorrowful sound
Aspiring for the freedom
Of the skies.
Once, but once, let it fly
And winter will pass
Into oblivion.
The world will be full
Of Spring and mirth.
Once, but once
Let it fly.

The eternal smile

A smile, which countless people have seen,
A painting, in the Louvre, Paris, for centuries has there been,
Painted by Da Vinci, the famous Mona Lisa stands,
Visited by millions, from near and far lands,
Her smile, once seen, lasts in memory for eternal time,
Such enigma, such charm, of a lady in her prime,
La Gioconda, her unheralded, unpretentious name,
Hailing from a family, of nobility. of some fame,
Her exotic, mysterious. enrapturing smile,
To all who watch her, does forever beguile,
The alluring nature of her smiling face,
Fills the mind with beauty and grace,
Posterity, ages hence shall stop every while,
And gaze entranced at the eternal smile.

Conquerors of a fractured world

Scavengers are they , urchins from the street ,
From early morning, with bags in hand , at rubbish dumps they
meet ,
Foraging for thrown away items, whatever they can find,
Little brothers and sisters, none are left behind;

The daily vistors to the garbage heaps are a motley mix,
Humans and creatures, all in a similar fix,
A family of hogs, goats, dogs and some timid bovine,
Sniffing around, sensing any morsel on which one can safely dine;

A litter of puppies, together six, follow their mother dear,
Each foraging, and playing with their sibling near,
A few days thence, there remained only three,
Some boys had taken the others home, to rear them for free;

On one cold night, nestled outside, a puppy would cry,
Few humans in their beds would ask the question why,
Born into a cruel world, the puppy decided to fight
In the adversarial world, together with the urchins that night;

A Birthday party in a large house brought many guests the same
night,
The next morning , some leftover food was offered to the urchins
in sight,
They ate a rare hearty meal, gathered around their grassy seat,
And kindly shared some plates with the onlooking dogs and the
puppies to eat;

Now the puppies roam, with bold hearts searching the waste,
The urchin boys and girls, with courage, saunter with no added haste,
Creatures and humans, like boats with sails, unfurled,
Heads held high, conquerors of a fractured world.

O Flower

Favorite of the gods, O flower of delightful creation,
Every petal of yours is a portal to heaven's domain,
The abode of enchantment, the pedestal of adulation,
Such beauty incomparable to any on this terrain ;

An entire world resides in you, O flower,
One filled with charms only dreams can inspire,
Where every bee in search of nectar in your fragrant bower
For unearthly realms do fervently aspire ;

For time immemorial humans have watched you in revered awe,
Innumerable gardens and homes do your presence adorn,
Your graceful image every artist strives to draw,
Your blooming smile enchants every creature in the early morn.

Dewdrops

Perhaps this early morn may hold a few dewdrops
Which would live till sunshine
Erased their lives and the transience
Would no longer be remembered -
The bees would hum along their way,
Oblivious of the death of the dewdrops,
Life would go on.

May it be, though, that somewhere,
In meticulous detail,
The lives of these drops of glistening dew
Have been recorded
And paeans to them have been sung -
Every life has been rejoiced,
Every death has been mourned?

The flow of time

As a river moves, time does flow,
Flowers, birds and nature do know,
The secret of time's existence in earth and space,
We frail humans the dilemmas of time face;

There is no time , some physicists avow,
The past, present and future are all happening now,
In parallel worlds exist parallel lives,
Each human in every different life thrives;

Time is nonlinear, many scientists reveal,
In our three dimensional universe time as an arrow flows, some feel,
To match the flow of time, body and age,
An active mind must we humans engage.

The hills of fluted song

In those hills clad in flourishing green
Standing below the clear azure sky,
The music of the flute flows serene,
 Mingles with the clouds and sails high;

The rocks stand in raptured stance
The woods remain in silent awe,
The grazing cattle cast a furtive glance,
Women carrying lumber step without a flaw;

Millions of years have passed since then
When the hills were born and raised with time,
The tribals came and settled in the glen,
And worshipped the hills with their song sublime ;

The music courses across the moonlit night,
And through the heart where it does belong,
Its note blends with the radiant twilight
And glides over the hills of fluted song.

The flower

How can a flower not bloom
Whether there be rain, hail or snow?
Why does a flower dispel the gloom
And set mournful faces aglow?

Why does a flower welcome the bird
To drink sweet nectar and sing?
Why does a flower spread the word
Of joy, and blissful tides bring?

The wind whispers, the eagle flies
And bees encircle the flower ;
Amidst the clouds, the answer lies
Etched in every drop of a shower.

The golden dawn

At night's end, when the black skies clear,
And birds begin their mellifluous songs,
The heart knows that glorious dawn is near,
In freedom's haste to reside with nature it longs;

The mind obliterates yesterday's woes and fears,
The wind blows in heightened delight,
Clear dewdrops remain on leaves as tears
Of happiness, as butterflies flutter with graceful birds in flight;

Sweet fragrance permeates the air with lightened ease,
Smiling blooms adorn plants in colored fest,
The fresh leaves of grass dance in the soft breeze,
Adorable garlands does nature weave in eager zest;

The morning brings new hopes for a novel day,
Animals walk in cherished steps in the incense breathing morn,
Sounds of life vibrate in rhythmless song,
Harking, heralding and ushering the golden dawn.

In Calicut (modern Kozikode), the flower Juhi-Hasnuhana (jasmine) is known as the flower of sorrow. The flower has been known since ancient times. When the Portuguese arrived in Calicut under Vasco da Gama in 1498, they saw the flower in the market place and elsewhere in the city. A sad tale is connected to the flower. The story has been told and retold for centuries. The poem relates the tragic tale of romance.

The flowers of sorrow

Heartbreaking and sad, of centuries ago, is a tale so dear,
Of a beautiful princess, the sole daughter of a king
Of Calicut, whose beauty spread far and near,
Suitors from every corner did her charms bring;

The perfect match for her in them she never found,
When earthly mortals to win her heart she failed to find,
She sought her love among gods heavenward bound,
And in the radiant and glorious Sun God she set her mind;

To answer the princess's prayers and fervent love,
The Sun God, moved, descended to Earth,
Showered with blessings and love from above,
The princess spent the night with the Sun God in mirth;

Yet at night's end, the Sun God left to rise as the dawn,
The princess was overcome with unrestrained grief,
Her eternal love had deserted her for the morn,
Her welling tears could never bring back the meeting so brief;

Ceaselessly in vain, she pined for her deity to return,
Till in deepened grief, she prepared her life to end,
The flames rose high as her remains did burn,
And the tragic message did the wind to the heavens send;

Her ashes fell on the bosom of the earth,
And mingled with the soil holy and free,
When the first drops of rain fell there with no dearth,
There grew and spread a lovely tree;

Beautiful flowers bloomed, colored orange and white,
Scattered over the grass, by the evening wind along,
Spreading the fragrance every starry night,
The leaves whispering an eternal love song ;

Yet when the sun appears with its morning light,
She hides, shy as a demure bride,
For she spreads her fragrance only at night,
To reveal her face in the morning she does deride;

The juhi hasnahana's tale of immortal love,
Lives with the night and shies away from the morrow,
The tree stands, watched in awe by the heavens above,
The sweet flowers bloom only at night, the magnificent flowers of
sorrow.

The little princess

The little princess-
She had colors on her facei,
The colors of Holi,
Dabbled
On her little cheeks by her brothers
Who ran around, spraying colors,
Leaving her standing in front
Of the Mall;
On the low walls of the boundary
She smeared colors with her hands;
People called her, the little one,
And talked to her,
They gave her some coins ;
She spoke to them, in child language,
Playing with the coins
Whose value she had no idea of ;
She asked others for more coins,
As she had been taught ;
They gave her some more and
In her sweet little voice
She conversed in halted language ;
Perhaps her parents lived nearby
In one of the street corners ;
Perhaps her brothers begged on the streets -
The innocent face, the innocent eyes ;
She walks towards an uncertain future
In a hostile world;
The little princess,
Her kingdom lies on the dust
Of the streets,
The little princess,

She is the youngest beggar in the streets
Of the Big City.

The local bazaar

The local bazaar, milieu of native crowd,
Where vendors haggle, in voices loud,
Wheeled carts, loaded with fruits of a different hue,
Country women, selling vegetables, fresh and new,
People moving, clad in garments of varying shade,
With eyes for produce profusely in baskets laid,
The meat seller standing beside his stall,
Chickens peeping from baskets, goats walking tall,
The fisherman arranges his fish upfront,
"200 Rs a kilo", he says with a grunt;
Cartsellers offer delicious oil fried food,
Crowds gather soon, the taste is so good,
A tea stall beside showcases sweets of sweetened delight,
Customers arrive in numbers, day and night,
Two grocery shops stand on the opposite side,
Women buy rice and lentils and all else beside,
Young riders on motorbikes ride carefree
Crowded on the seat, a total of three,
On the crowded road, cars honk and sail,
Dodging other vehicles, as road rules fail,
The cacophony reverberates, rising to a din,
The argot of the market, flowing from within,
Vendors head home with the end of the day,
The cart sellers remain, as people pause to eat on their way,
As the night lamps glow with dimming light,
Silence falls, beneath the starlit night.

The lost deity

A temple stands, in ruined glory,
An architectural marvel of ancient years,
The gates, the columns that remain tell a story,
Of ceremonies grand and flowing tears;

In days of yore, devout pilgrims all,
Climbed atop on the carved steps galore,
To see a deity in the sanctimonious inner hall,
And pay obeisance for blessings and more;

Time and humans ravaged the temple's hallowed mounds
And caused the deity, its splendor and grandeur to depart,
Yet the beautiful ruins which remain speak in silent sounds,
The past and present remain a world apart;

Magnificent carvings, amidst the ruins that bemoan,
Empty and silent now, the deity none can find
Among the broken altars, pillars and ornate stone,
The lost deity remains entrenched in the pilgrims heart and mindp.
The Lost Deity

A temple stands, in ruined glory,
An architectural marvel of ancient years,
The gates, the columns that remain tell a story,
Of ceremonies grand and flowing tears;

In days of yore, devout pilgrims all,
Climbed atop on the carved steps galore,
To see a deity in the sanctimonious inner hall,
And pay obeisance for blessings and more;

Time and humans ravaged the temple's hallowed mounds
And caused the deity, its splendor and grandeur to depart,
Yet the beautiful ruins which remain speak in silent sounds,
The past and present remain a world apart;

Magnificent carvings, amidst the ruins that bemoan,
Empty and silent now, the deity none can find
Among the broken altars, pillars and ornate stone,
The lost deity remains entrenched in the pilgrims heart and mind.

The hibiscus

Red as the sun at dawn, bathed in sunshine all day,
The hibiscus with joyous vibes with the wind does sway,
Lustrous sun-loving blossoms in colors beautiful and many,
Enlightening a summer garden even when the day is rainy,
Butterflies, hummingbirds hover to receive its nectar delight,
The beauty of the hibiscus is an awe-inspiring, picturesque sight.

The lost river

Oft mentioned in the hallowed Rig Veda
Lauded with hymns in Indra's demesne,
The fount of wisdom. radiant goddess,
Sarasvati, the mighty river of ancient lore,
Bountiful, nurturer of lofty civilization,
On your consecrated ancient banks
Were the revered Vedas composed ;
Beside your copious flow, magnificent
cities grew,
Grandiloquent in bearing, Barnawali, Lothal,
Kalibangan, Dholavira and scores of others
Exalted in construction and layout,
Exemplary in planning in every detail;
Ships trading beyond the shores of the nation
To distant kingdoms , Mesopotamia and Egypt
Laden with the exquisite goods of Meluha ;
The Seven Sister rivers of which you are one,
O Goddess, of unbridled knowledge,
You nurtured the Indus Saraswati civilization
Mohenjo Daro, Harappa and your cities
Rose to dizzying heights of technology
With a script on its inimitable seals
Still undeciphered, mystifying generations
Who gazed in awe and stupefaction ;
The fallen heroes of the Mahabharata
Were cremated on your sacred banks ;
The great war was fought within your sight ;
Balaram, the brother of Krishna,
Traveled along your banks on pilgrimage
To resplendent cities that defied time
And grew in splendor even as you dwindled ;

When the Shatudri became the Shatadru
And left your blessed banks to join the Indus,
The Yamuna separated to join the Ganges,
As you gradually dried and much disappeared,
People of the once golden civilization
Now decayed, migrated north. east, west
And South
Towards the Ganges and the Indus,
To the Narmada and the Tapti,
You became a living memory ;
O daughter of Brahma, your unseen hand
Shapes our minds, our civilization now
And shall forever bear your blessings;
Hail to thee O Goddess,
Immortal Sarasvati, source of wisdom,
Guide of humankind, for eternity.

The morning fog

Fog descends in the early morn on the earth,
The veil of mystery on nature's alluring face,
Through the mists the bird's song of mirth
Floats gaily across, with elegance and grace;
O transient visitor, whom do you seek
Amidst scattered blossoms, this early morn?
The sun with diffidence is today meek
And the flowers slumber as if not yet born ;
The winter's wind, from the shrouded hills
Pause at your steps, bowing with esteem,
The ambience with solemn wonder and hope fills,
The obscure present shall the future redeem.

The mind

The body is unable, but the mind can fly,
Fetters of life it breaks open and soars
To heights, in the realms of the sun and sky
To distances, along known and unknown shores;

The desires of the heart the mind does fulfill,
To the moon and stars does it sail,
Down the fathoms, tranquil and still,
It traverses realms of mystery, without fail;

None can harness the powers of the mind, it may seem,
As the wind travels, in all directions and free,
The mind sails, in wakefulness and dream
With the wings of time and the crown of victory.

The festival of colors

When spring adorns the garb of a spectrum of colors under the
sun
All rejoice with joy as the Festival of Colors has begun,
Flying in the air, the sight and aroma of every hue
The heart does mirthfully inspire, the mind does wholesomely
imbue,
Children and adults in the streets, with colors smeared on every
face,
The music of colors sails from Krishna›s enchanted flute with
grace,
Green, blue, yellow, red, all float in the air, each with a dream,
The panorama of life, bathed in magical smiles does seem;
Affluent or impoverished, differences in humanity together as one
melt,
Unity amidst diversity, the Festival of Colors in all hearts is
cherishingly felt.

The Old Barber

Stooping low, with slow steps, the old barber walks,
An old box in his hand, a bottle of oil,
A withered hand, a pair of old shoes on his feet,
He trudges towards a few houses, to give a haircut
A manicure, a neck massage, in the traditional style,
The little money he earns gives him bare subsistence,
He lives with his aged wife of many fond years ;
His cadaver like eyes reflect past memories of days behind,
With halting steps the old man walks towards the future;
A travelling barber, he owns no shops
As the younger generations now do ;
Visions of better times appear before his eyes,
His two sons are away, living in another state,
His married daughter who he longs to see lives far;
Through the jumbled lanes the barber walks, in unhurried slow
steps,
The past lingers in his eyes, the future a haunting melody,
Time a dwindling commodity, hope a desire,
The old barber walks in eloquent silence.

The eyes of thine

Whereupon the eyes of Thine,
In joy or sorrow meet with mine,
Every turn of life will seem
The realization of a beautiful dream ;
Wherever in my journeys I may be,
Your image and countenance I will see ;
Every night the stars in the sky
With radiance of yours shall forever lie;
In my mind and in my heart,
Etched in gold, it shall never depart.

The peacock

Magnificent bird, with delightful plume,
Your presence and dance dispels every gloom,
Your feathers spread in fantastic grace,
The charms of your eyes does every human amaze,
The nation's pride, you walk in state,
As a bird emerging from heaven's gate,
Your crest a symbol of nobility, a crowning sail,
Wonders in turquoise and gold sparkle on your treasured tail,
The seat of a god, you reside in pleasant paradise,
A dazzling spectacle must you be, a divinity in disguise.

Dreams

Strands of clouds hovering over the expansive blue,
Fragmented dreams, floating over a lost realm
Like derelict ships
Laden with treasures of mortal humans
Sans pilot, perennial peripatetics,
Who would dare to reach- who would dare
To bring them to earth
Only to collide with reality›s harshness?

The photograph

A photograph stares in
fixed gaze -
A smile I knew during my childhood: years ;
A smile that years have not erased
That also among the stars resides;
Those silent travelers, with lamps in hand
March across the skies, and there
I sense the smile, the intensity
Not diminished after all these years -
Now amidst the crowded twinkling members
Which the constellations bear
Is a face which fond memories do extend
Across limitless barriers;
Years of wandering through life›s murky streams
Over streaks of graying hair have not waned
The memories of care, of a bygone life
Where youth leaped under the security
Of a fond home, now that home resides
In the Universe, and it›s reflection
In the stream by moonlight,
Hanging from the wall, ‹tis more
Than a photograph - life still stares
Beyond the frames, A living smile,
Not a plaintive melody,
A joyous caressing from a world beyond.

The rose flower

May the rose every garden adorn,
Unmitigated beauty, in every blossom born,
The fragrance that spreads, in the mist and air
Inspires lyrics of poetry extolled in words so fair ;
Every rose shall humans forever praise,
Viewing each petal in unperturbed gaze;
The rose is real, the rose is a dream,
Without its charms, life futile may seem,
Paragon of creation, nature's immaculate art,
O rose flower you are the gift from the Divine heart.

The wind

The wind can be high and mighty, or a billowy breeze
Or icy cold, where life would slowly freeze;
In a gail or storm the wind is furious and fast,
Beside the sea, the breeze from the water would long last;
The summer wind brings a tide of heat,
In spring the fair wind do the flowers meet;
The autumn wind changes leaves to flowers in color,
The wind blows through houses of the rich and those of squalor;
In the woods the wind rustles past the leaves so green,
The mountain wind climbs to the clouds and in between;
The home of the wind perhaps, the wind only knows,
It dwells in unearthly realms from where every wind blows.

The starry night

Standing on the balcony, starry eyed, I see
 Countless points of light, twinkling in harmony,
Constellations spread in patterned geometrical design
As far as they can see, these eyes of mine;

The moon lights the paths to the earth and to the woods,
Clouds wander, in obscure and revealing moods,
Water in the stream shimmers in the light,
Birds are asleep, the wind awakens to an exuberant night;

City lights brighten, competing with the stars,
The moon shines with the romance of being,
The air is filled with the sounds of tankers, trucks, bikes and cars,
Imagination under the illuminated night soars with a wing ;

Frail beings we seem in the universe so vast in sight,
The earth a blue dot in far space would appear
Under the heavens, a shelter so soothing and bright,
The starry night in our hearts and minds we eternally endear.

The silent snowflakes

Silent snowflakes fall in the quiet woods
Like cotton wool floating in elegant dance,
Bare trees watch in silent awe,
Bent branches on trunks rooted in snow,
The ground, white as a sheet for miles around,
Not even a lonely fox appears in the distance,
Nature, in muted silence performs the melody
For a universal symphony, the flowing wind
Adds to the music with a low whistle ;
Can you hear the silent song of the snowflakes, O traveller,
The voices of life and hope in this forsaken, tranquil realm?

The riverbank

The serene riverbank
No sound of broken hearts
No cries of stressed minds around,
Just a leaf fluttering
From a solitary tree,
Dancing
To the rhythms of life,
No passion, only dreams
Of a world past its slumbers;
Listening to the rippling water
And basking in the sunshine
Away from life's daily woes;
A fish leaps out of the water
It's scales slanted against the sun;
Shining, reflecting. shimmering ,
A moment of joy
Then returns to its world again.

The footsteps of eternity

The sunsets and awakens the Eternal Mind,
The silhouette of life, does in the reflected waters rest,
Footsteps of eternity does in every moment find
The touch of perfection, blessed at nature's behest.

The tree of destiny

Somewhere, in some realm, where the air is pristine and free,
Standing on a hillock is the tree of destiny;
In the early dawn, beneath the flowing blue in sight,
The tree is discerned, by dawn's early light;
There it stands, with humankind's hopes and fears,
Bearing all life's vicissitudes, all joys and tears;
The calm breeze blows by, as if a watery stream,
Touching the tree with every desire, every wishful dream;
The rustling leaves carry whispers from every human heart,
Every life is preserved within and shall never depart:
The murmurs of every mind to a crescendo rises as the day rolls by,
The clouds listen, as they sail across the azure sky,
At night's end, when twinkling stars towards the dawn unwind,
Every dream vibrates with visions of the future of humankind.

The rose garden

Where the fresh fragrance of the rose flows
And the billowy breeze brings memories home,
In that rose garden the lamp in the heart glows
And clouds of dreams freely roam.

The neoclassical Italian sculptor Giovani Belzoni created The Veiled Rebecca in 1863. It depicts the biblical character Rebecca, wife of Isaac (son of Abraham) who veiled herself on meeting her future husband. The sculptor's artistry and high level of skill are evident in the stone as a fabric covering the body with folds chiselled with such skill that it appears real. A veiled woman during those times had become an allegory for Italian unification.

Benzoni›s workshop made a number of copies, one of which is in the Salar Jung Museum in Hyderabad, in India.

A few lines on the famous sculpted image are presented below:

The veiled rebecca

Melody in marble, a sculptor molded you as a fount of mystery,
You remain cherished in the sacred vaults of history,
Carved in stone, veiled, as you stood before Isaac, immaculate art,
Cloth folded in stone, did Benzoni adroitly insert,
Your face, hidden yet alive, millions of watchers admire,
A countenance that blessed tales inspire,
Every awestruck voice your enigmatic grace does ponder,
You remain, a perennial source of mystery and wonder,
For eternity, O Rebecca, would you remain behind the veil,
Your sacred story shall repeatedly tell.

Cherry blossoms

Pink cherry blossoms, beneath the sky so blue,
A narrow winding road, beside the manicured green grass,
Clouds sailing by, in spirits free and true,
The wind a fresh aroma brings to pass;

Spring is here, in colors varied and sweet,
Emerging fresh leaves sway with vigor anew,
Smiling blossoms the jubilant heart they meet,
Blessed with nature›s melody and panoramic view;

Standing below the flowers with the clouds the mind dreams,
As the gates of paradise open their hallowed doors,
A kingdom spread with beauteous bounty seems,
The cherry blossoms' fragrance to heaven soars.

Where the mind fears to tread

Where the mind fears to tread,
The heart does not ;
It traverses the unheralded paths of dread
That the world forgot;
Now shines the heart's radiant light,
As the migrant birds alight in flight,
And shall the heart speak to the mind,
To soar forward into the hearts of humankind;
Listen to the afflicted, listen to those
Whom society with false pride to ignore, chose,
Listen to their grief, their voices smothered by the world's insanity,
Bring to them the luminous light of humanity.

The earth and the sky

The earth beneath the sky
The sky beyond the earth
Have you listened
To their voices?

Have you heard
The cries of millions
The agonies spread
Through the ether?

Have you seen
The tears
Shining down
The face of history?

Have you felt
The joys of union
The pangs
Of separation
The longing for peace?

Have you sensed
The juggernaut
Of destruction
Rolling over
The multitudes
A pageant
Of death
Across the ages?

Have you believed
That life rejoices
Amidst
The sorrows
In the quest
For freedom
Of the mind
For humanity?

A view from the barbed fence

From the barbed fence, a house appears,
Dilapidated, with obsolete doors, windows,
Tree roots climbing down its floors,
Open cavities in walls
At the mercy of the capricious wind
And nature's elements in gleeful conquest;
Inside, empty dreams remain afloat,
Of past glories, sorrows and joys,
Voices, a cacophony of whispers
Drowning the silence of trees around;
Strains of music hover in the insipid air-
Does someone weep?
Whose agonizing cries arise,
Aspiring for freedom from the stone walls?
Listen again, do you not hear
Sounds of mirth and laughter
Amidst people gathered in the once long hall?
The tinkling of ankle bells, sounds
Of instruments of percussion and wind,
Stringed melodies wandering in the ears?
Do you not hear the sound of horses' hooves
The wheels of carriages grinding to a halt,
Conversations of people entering
And leaving in casual gaiety,
Or smell the fragrance of culinary delights
Mingling with the smoke of the past,
Melodies, voices of hope and anguish
A cadence that ebbs and flows
With time's honored moments
In tumultuous profusion?

Pause for a while, weary traveler
And traverse the tortured paths
Through the portals of time,
Linger, O traveler, for a view
From the barbed fence.

A stream in the woods

A clearing in the woods, along a dusty road I walk,
With turns aside the bushes till I come across a rock,
Protruding flat, above a gorge amidst rocky terrain,
Below, a thin stream of water cutting through the domain ;
Dense foliage on the other side of the stream,
Tranquil, save the sound of some birds, so divine does seem;
Thousands of years, perhaps millions the earth has seen
Since the ancient forest arose, pristine and green,
The stream when full of water from the rain, gurgles and flows,
Speaking in a language which nobody knows,
Every moment in the quiet yet eloquent woods
Is a vibrant, tender smile from nature's joyous moods.

9 789390 640577